THE
CHRISTMAS TREE
Its Spiritual Meaning

THE
CHRISTMAS TREE
Its Spiritual Meaning

Written by BARRY BRUNSMAN
Illustrations by ARDIS J. BOW

For information on purchasing additional copies of this book please contact:
Special Ministries
P.O. Box 340026, Sacramento, CA 95834-0026
1-800-293-5400

design & layout: martinez/hardy design & communication

DEDICATION

To all the children of the world

especially for those who need to know

how beautiful they are.

FOREWARD

A HINDU NAMED HATAR SINGH JOURNEYED TO THE UNITED STATES. It was Christmas time. He and his family were graciously welcomed into the home of a Christian family in Chicago. Upon entering the home, the visitors from India were enchanted by the sight of an exquisitely decorated fir tree standing in the corner of the living room. In perfect English, Hatar asked, "Do you plant trees in houses here? This is a custom I've not heard of! What is the significance of all these beautiful decorations?" The hostess replied, "Oh, no, this is a cut tree from a Christmas tree farm. The decorations are a custom we do during the Christmas season."

Still curious, Hatar inquired, "Where did the custom come from, and what do these wonderful trinkets mean?" Somewhat embarrassed and lost for a meaningful explanation, the hostess answered, "I believe the custom began in Europe around the time of Saint Nicholas, and the decorations have evolved since then to make it more festive."

Of all the beautiful stories told during the Yuletide season, the Christmas tree tells one of the most enchanting. Its origin and decorations have very significant meanings.

The Origin

The year was about 724. It began in the center of Germany in a wooded area called Geismar. One freezing cold winter night in December the tribal people gathered around the great thunder oak that stood majestically among all the trees of the area. The people believed their gods, Thor and Odin, lived within that tree. The fires of worship flickered in a circle around the base of the magnificent tree. But instead of the worship of dance and song, there was a mournful prayer. People were sad. Some were crying. The Teutonic tribe believed their god, Thor, could only be satisfied with a human sacrifice. This time the handsome son of the chieftain was to become the victim.

☆

With knife poised on high, ceremoniously he walked toward the bound and terrified boy for the sacrificial kill.

The tribal priest bowed and chanted before the great thunder oak as if talking to the god, Thor, in the tree. The knife he was holding reflected with a flash in the golden glow of the fires as he danced about.

The priest stopped. With knife poised on high, ceremoniously he walked toward the bound and terrified boy for the sacrificial kill. Suddenly a commanding yell came from a charging figure emerging from the forest. "Stop! God does not want the death of this boy. God wants him to live." An audible sigh of approval rose from the worshippers.

The stately figure then addressed the chief of the tribe. He announced to everyone that his name was Boniface. He was a Christian. With confidence, Boniface proclaimed to all present that it was at this very time of the year that the great God of the heavens permitted a child to be born. That child was God's own. God wanted life, not death.

While the stunned priest stood in shocked attention, Boniface began to untie the boy. While loosening the bonds of the lad, Boniface told the story of the birth of Jesus in Bethlehem. He would be the Savior of all people. Jesus had come to save this boy. Boniface then led the young man to his mother and chieftain father who were crying for joy.

Boniface then said that their gods, Thor and Odin, knew the great God of the heavens. So that the tribe's people would not defy their gods, Boniface would chop down the great thunder oak. If their gods did not approve, they would strike him dead as he felled the tree.

Some say that as Boniface began to chop at the great thunder oak, a bolt of lightning struck the tree splitting it in half. Others say that Boniface chopped down the tree. Whichever it was, the people knew God did not want the death of the chief's son.

Aware of the people's love of nature, Boniface placed a fir tree on the stump of the great thunder oak. Boniface told them the fir tree represented the tree of good and evil in the Garden of Eden. He went

on to explain that when humans chose evil, God promised that a divine child would be born to help all people to choose good. So Boniface made the new tree to stand for God's promise, the promise of the divine son who came to make all people special. So the Christmas tree is a symbol of the Messiah who has come among us.

The origin of the word *Christmas* is slightly complicated. *Christos* means the anointed one, or Messiah. *Mas* or *Mass* is an action word. It is derived from the Latin word *mittere*, to send. The past tense is *missus*, sent. Taken together, the word Christmas means Messiah sent.

The Decorations

The decorations tell the story of the thrilling relationship God has with all people. It's the story the Son of God told so that people would have the good news first hand.

There are several decorations that crown the tree top. The oldest is the candle that simply announced that Christ is the supreme light of the world. The six-point star is the star of David. When this is used, everyone is reminded of the prophecies of the Hebrew scriptures that told about the coming of the Messiah. The Christians call these books the Old Testament. The five-point star is the star of Bethlehem. This star led the first Gentiles, the astrologers in the East, to know the Messiah was for them as well. On the other hand, when

☆

. . . WHEN THE TREE IS TOPPED BY AN ANGEL, IT PROCLAIMS THE PEACE THAT FILLED THE HEAVENS WHEN THE SAVIOR WAS BORN.

the tree is topped by an angel, it proclaims the peace that filled the heavens when the Savior was born.

The long, gold or silver streamers that originate at the very top of the tree and weave down and around to its base symbolize the divine presence or the divine grace that comes down from God to each person at baptism. The popcorn streamer has a similar meaning. One can imagine a grandparent taking the time to make and string popcorn with an impressionable young child all the while explaining that each little kernel of popped corn represents some wonderful gift or grace that God had given to that little one.

The tree ornaments or decorations come from many different cultures. Originally the only ornament was round and red, reminding us of the apple from the tree in Eden. In fact, on occasion, Christmas trees are decorated with artificial red apples. In the tropics people could not relate to the red fruit so the ornament took on the color of yellow. In other areas, green, orange and even blue told the story of when the Redeemer was first promised.

The trinkets and figurines on the tree are traceable to the Jesse tree. Several of the massive cathedrals of Europe have the Jesse tree adorning the stained glass windows. The ornaments tell of the awe-

some history that preceded and predicted the arrival of the Messiah. Jesse was the father of David. From the house of David would come the Messiah. The Jesse tree was often a gaunt looking tree with seven branches, each with a candle or light affixed to the top. These branches were decorated with figurines representing the tablets of the law, the key of David, Bethlehem, the root of Jesse, Noah's ark, the rod of Aaron, manna, the burning bush, the pillar of fire, the sword of Judith, Jacob's ladder, the Ark of the Covenant, the altar of the holocaust, the apple, Jonah and the whale, the Temple, and the crown and scepter. In a similar tradition, the Christian community often decorated the Christmas tree with small loaves of bread for communion, oil for anointing, the cross for forgiveness, and a vial of water for baptism.

In different parts of the world, creative Christian communities would decorate the Christmas tree with symbols representing many other sacred gifts that God had given them. Each family member would fashion a symbol of the talent he or she saw in their mother, father, sister, or brother. Every Sunday of Advent each would place an ornament symbol on the tree to express appreciation to God for the gifts of other members of the family. Examples might include a drawing of a smile for an individual with a sense of humor, a hammer for the fix-it person, a paint brush for an artist. By the time Christmas arrived, there was a heightened awareness of all the gifts that God had granted to that family because of each person present.

The tinsel often has been associated with the images of snow and icicles. This symbol is embedded in an early Christian concept that every follower of Jesus Christ is showered with God's blessings, much like snow or rain falling on someone. With this in mind, a person looking at the tinsel hanging from the branches of the Christmas tree would have some idea of the favors God rains on each individual every moment of life. Martin Luther seems to have added this touch.

Candles originally adorned the trees. Often they were lit from the single candle that mounted the top of the tree, much like at the Easter Vigil with the prominence of the Christ candle. There were as many candles on the tree as there were members of the household. Each was lit from the Christ candle at the top. The candles on the fir tree were obviously a fire danger. The first reported use of electric light bulbs on the Christmas tree was in 1909 in Pasadena, California. At first these lights were all white, imitating the candles of former years. As time went by, the lights became multi-colored. Without a doubt, those with imagination rejoiced at the uniqueness of each bulb as people have different personalities. Still, each bulb was lit by the same electricity (divine energy) which would symbolize for many the uniqueness of each individual made bright by the same grace of Christ Jesus.

THE GIFTS

THE GIFTS UNDER THE TREE TELL A SLIGHTLY DIFFERENT STORY. In the near East, Turkey, Lebanon, Syria, Greece, and other countries, gifts are exchanged on December 6th, the Feast of Saint Nicholas, who was the bishop of Myra in Southern Turkey in the early part of the fourth century. He was known for taking care of poor children, especially destitute girls. In those parts of the world, gifts were given primarily to the poor, a growing custom in many Christian communities in the United States. "Good ole St. Nick" would become Santa Claus in the 1700s in the Western part of the

☆

SANTA CLAUS WEARS THE CLOTHING OF THE BISHOP –
A BISHOP FOR THE POOR.

world. Santa Claus wears the clothing of the bishop – a bishop for the poor. Every gift is meant to recall God's generous gift of the Messiah. Christmas presents originally had the message, "From the Christ in me to the Christ in you!"

In many of the Latin American countries, gifts are given on the 6th of January, the feast day of when the Magi brought their gifts of gold, frankincense and myrrh to the infant of Bethlehem. In other Western countries, gifts are exchanged on Christmas eve or Christmas morning.

For many centuries there were several images of the baby Jesus. Most of these were mosaics or paintings on the walls of churches and chapels or on sheep skins. Most featured the child alone. Sometimes the baby was dressed in priestly or kingly robes and other times in swaddling clothes. Occasionally there were images of mother, child and Joseph. However, in 1223 the vibrant and imaginative Francis of Assisi wanted to celebrate Christmas in the town of Greccio, Italy. He was a down-to-earth, yet romantic and dramatic individual. So the people of the area might appreciate the humanity and birth conditions of the Savior, Francis enlisted the help of the town's people to enact the entire Bethlehem scene. With real people and animals,

he led a candlelight procession to one of the caves in the mountains nearby. It was here that he laid the image of the infant child in a manger, amid the singing of the town's people. This proved to be so real and moving that the pageant soon was reenacted in villages and towns throughout Europe. From this came the nativity scene with statues of people and animals. In many countries the Crèche (crib) is placed beneath the Christmas tree.

Figurines are found in the oldest cultures discovered in archeology. However, in recent centuries, dolls seem to have originated from the Christ child figurine. In the early 1600s there was a movement against images in the form of statuary. The daughter of a German woodcarver did not understand the concerns of the adults. At the end of the Christmas season, she continued to play with the little figurine of the child Jesus. Her playmates wanted one as well.

The woodcarver began to produce other dolls like that of his daughter's. Soon the dolls were being dressed in the ethnic attire of children in that area. The popularity of the Christ child dolls spread quickly. Certainly it would come as a great surprise to know that the origin of the Barbie® doll was from the child Jesus in the manger.

Prologue

The Christmas tree and its decorations tell a profoundly beautiful story. The tale of a rich, revealing history. It highlights the treasure-trove of talents and gifts given to each and every person celebrating the birth of the Son of God. The story of how the Creator God so loved the world as to send Jesus Christ to live among the people as the supreme example of love and light, of intimacy and healing.

During his Chicago stay, Hatar, our Hindu visitor, missed hearing the greatest event ever told as his hostess was unaware of the rich, spiritual meaning of the Christmas tree.